LIFE AFTER CLOSING

SHEA C. JOHNSON

The links or hyperlinks in this book are provided as a convenience for informational purposes only. They do not constitute an endorsement nor an approval by the author of this book of any of the products, services or opinions of the owners, creators, individuals, organizations and/or authors of the links provided. The author bears no responsibility for the accuracy, legality, continued existence, or content of the external site or for that of subsequent links. Links were assessed and verified at the time of publication in the format provided but may subsequently be altered, removed, or become extinct at any time at no notification, control, or liability of the author of this book. Please contact site owners for answers to questions regarding its content.

This publication contains ideas, opinions, and personal experiences of its author. It is sold with the understanding that neither the publisher nor the author is engaged in rendering legal, tax, investment, financial, insurance, accounting, or other professional advice or services. The information in this book may not be applicable in all states, jurisdictions, or communities. Some information may have become outdated after this book was written.

Copyright © 2022 Shea C. Johnson

All Rights Reserved. No part of this publication may be reproduced or transmitted, stored in a retrieval system, or transmitted in any form or by any means, electronic, mechanical, photocopying, recording, scanning, or otherwise, except as permitted by law, without prior written permission of the author.

Printed in the United States of America

Editor: Sharp Editorial, LLC

Cover Design: JD&J Design LLC

Book Interior Illustrations: Shea C. Johnson

DEDICATION

To my husband, Tink: Thank you for your constant encouragement in all my endeavors. Thanks for always being my calm within the storm. This is just the beginning of more great things to come for us.

To Daiee: Thank you for being all that you are and for teaching me all there is to know about everything hands-on when it comes to a house... and more. Thank you for motivating and preparing me by buying me my very first drill. Thanks for being *so* smart and for making everything look *so* easy.

To Ma: I am your "Jr." If we did not have the desire to invest and take the real estate class together, I'm not sure where I would be today. No matter how crazy my ideas might be, you always encourage me to try anyway. Thank you for always being by my side as my biggest cheerleader.

To Muffy and Ian: Thank you for being such great kids. You will probably never know how many ideas you have inspired in my life. Thank you for being patient with me while I run in 100 different directions.

To Nina Bean: Your grand entrance motivated me to stop procrastinating and reminded me of the preciousness of time.

I always strive to do more and to be more, solely because of you six.

I also dedicate this book to every client who has bought or sold a house with me and to everyone who has ever referred a client my way. I am truly humbled, and I appreciate you more than you will ever know. Referrals are the highest compliment I could ever receive. Every referral I receive lets me know how you feel about my knowledge, service, and dedication in my line of work. I am now and will forever be extremely grateful.

Thank you.

TABLE OF CONTENTS

Introduction 8
Ten Important Steps After Closing 15
Warranty vs. Homeowner Insurance 23
Homeowner Association, Condo,
and Front-Foot Benefit Fees 30
Call Before You Dig 35
Plumbing 37
What is a Grinder Pump? 41
Well and Septic 42
Roof and Gutters 51
Grading 53
Foundation or Settlement Cracks 54
Moisture Infiltration and Damage 57
What is a Sump Pump? 63
Electrical 65
Heating Ventilation & Air Conditioning (HVAC) 68
Boiler Heating Systems 71
Flooring 72
General Maintenance 74
Utilities 78

Go Green at Home	84
Uninvited Guests	87
Title Insurance	90
Adding a Spouse/Significant Other to a Deed	92
Financial Issues After Buying	95
What If I Have a Reverse Mortgage?	98
What If I Need to Sell?	100
What If I Don't Have Equity?	102
Security	106
Your Home is Your Castle	110
References	113
About the Author	117
Appendix	118

INTRODUCTION

Over the course of my 24 years of selling real estate, several buyers have come to me after closing on their first home and asked, "What do I do now? I've bought the home... now what?" This question prompted me to write this book. There are thousands of books on the market that teach buyers and sellers what to do before buying a home. Many books teach how to make offers and how to invest. Other than complicated do-it-yourself handbooks, I could not find any guides that specifically target *you*, the new buyer, the one who has made his or her dream come true and now needs a little help in understanding what to do next.

In this book, I discuss more than the schematics that amass a home. I help to make sense of many aspects involving owning a home and protecting your investment. I hope to bring comfort and peace of mind by making the world of homeownership clear and easy. I will discuss specificities involving various areas of a home, including, but not limited to, the interior, the exterior, and utilities. Purchasing a home is a huge step in a person's life, regardless of whether it's your first purchase. Each transaction is unique, and each house is unique. Some homeowners may have owned a home for years and still have questions. Some buyers may be on the fence at the beginning of their home search because purchasing a home can seem like such an overwhelming step. I've had buyers tell me, "I'm scared. What if I don't know what to do?" I have heard this so often in my career that I felt it was a *must* to write this book.

Initially, I wanted to design a short pamphlet to provide to my first-time homebuyers at closing to help them feel more comfortable when making a purchase. I yearn for buyers to be comfortable, and I have a deep desire for them to understand what to do *after* closing. Then, I decided that there must be other buyers in the world who also need this information. This book addresses many unanswered questions that new and long-time homeowners have after making a purchase.

Buying a home is one of the most important steps in a person's life and sometimes the largest purchase a person or family will ever make in their lifetime. Before purchasing a house, I always suggest that buyers hire a competent home inspector to inspect a home and all its major components to determine if the repairs needed are too costly for the buyer's budget. An inspector's duty is not to determine *if* there is something in disrepair in a home because there is almost always an item in need of repair. I suggest inspections so that buyers can discover the home's current condition; hence, what items may need to be repaired. Buyers should not expect sellers to make everything new based on the findings of an inspection. There will always be repair items uncovered in all inspected homes, regardless of the quality of the home's construction, so these should not come as a surprise to any buyer.

Every home will need repairs at some point in time. Even the White House needs repairs periodically. Do not let this deter you. Determining a home's condition helps you know what is needed in advance to make an informed decision based on those needs. Consider if the repairs are too expensive for you—if so, maybe this is not the house for you. Your home inspection experience should be considered an informational journey. If you are thinking of selling, consider having a home inspection completed in advance to prepare your home for the market. As a seasoned agent, after being licensed for many years, I discuss this with buyers upfront. I often refer to a house with everything the buyer is looking for but still needs a few repairs as a Bentley. For those who are not familiar, a Bentley is an expensive luxury car. I tell buyers not to miss out on their Bentley because of a ding in the door. If a house fits all the buyer's needs and they decide to cancel a deal because of ridiculously small findings on a home inspection, I question the buyer's motivation. I question if they *really* love the home. If a buyer ruffles feathers over a doorknob or sticky cabinet, perhaps they are not truly motivated about that house. It has been my experience that small signs like this have led to a buyer canceling or being unhappy with their purchase. I want buyers to love the home they choose to buy. The likelihood of finding a home with fewer repairs than a doorknob or sticky cabinet in the next house is an unrealistic expectation.

If you are reading this book before you buy a home, note that requesting repairs while in contract negotiation may be considered a counteroffer, which re-opens your contract, potentially running the risk of a seller canceling your deal.

Consult your agent to devise the best strategy to handle your repair negotiations. Once you have closed on your home, there is most likely no further responsibility for the real estate agent or broker to assist, other than to keep details of your transaction confidential. The property's condition, the mortgage, and the awnings over the front door are all yours once you close. A good agent will try their best to continue to assist you after closing by answering questions you may have about your new purchase, but they are limited to any power beyond that. No further negotiating power exists beyond closing. If you discover defects you believe were hidden or not disclosed to you by the seller and that should or could have been revealed to you during your buying process, discuss this with your agent. Your agent can then suggest contacting a regulating office or an attorney.

In most areas, there are rules regulating how sellers disclose a property's condition that may penalize them or their agent for blatantly hiding or misrepresenting latent defects or material facts. A material fact is information that could have interfered with or influenced your decision to buy. Two examples of material facts are knowledge of an impending railroad track being constructed close to the house or Homeowner Association restrictions and bylaws. The following are *not* latent defects or material facts:

    A. You do not like the style of curtain rods used to hang drapes.

    B. The kitchen cabinets are too small to fit your pots and pans.

    C. There are not enough USB ports to charge your cell phones.

Those are just a few examples of items considered to be personal preferences. These examples are irrelevant to a home's condition and habitability. They should not have been deal-breakers for your decision to purchase because these items could be changed or modified after you close on the home. True latent defects would be a leaking pipe or a recurring or past mold concern. If your contract with the seller allows you to renegotiate and request repairs, it is customary to request items you feel would be out of your capacity to repair.

Homes are like cars. They constantly require maintenance to prevent major breakdowns, and issues can arise unexpectedly, as they often do with vehicles. However, with proper maintenance, as with a car, you can prevent and lessen your expenses by following the advice on maintenance in the manufacturer's manual. Regardless of your home's condition when you purchase it, good or bad, there will be instances when repairs will need to be made. Things happen, big and small, and this book will help prepare you for the most common problems that can occur after closing. I have included many homeowners' experiences, and I often wonder why someone did not tell them these issues could happen. As Benjamin Franklin once said, "An ounce of prevention is worth a pound of cure."

If you are reading this before you purchase a home, know that your inspection may also help you understand how systems operate in the home. Give your inspector both space and your undivided attention. Utilize a pad and pen to take notes. To avoid distraction, bar family members, pets, and anyone who is not on your contract from your inspection. Be respectful of the homeowner.

Whether the home is vacant or occupied, the house continues to be the seller's property until after closing. You and your agent could be held responsible for damages to the seller's property during an inspection.

I also like to compare the systems and structure of a home to the human body. Like the human body, a home is designed with parts, appliances, and systems that are constantly running to ensure that the home functions properly and keeps us comfortable. Just as the lungs breathe and the heart beats without cranking them to work, so does your furnace, refrigerator, air conditioning unit, roof, and foundation. The siding or brick exterior of a house represents human skin. It protects the inside from the outside. Systems that constantly run or sustain with motors or power can also wear out or need maintenance, require repairs, or eventually be replaced.

This book will assist you with a wealth of information by teaching you what to do after buying a home. This book also includes many fun ideas from my experience working as a real estate salesperson and private investor. No part of this book advises replacing hiring a licensed professional to access and diagnose possible damages and perform repairs. In no way should any of my opinions be interpreted as tax or legal advice. I assume no liability if the methods in this book do not provide desirable or satisfying results. The information and ideas in this book are solely my opinions. I'm sure many reading this book have handy skills and maybe a friend or family member who may challenge all my suggestions on how to get things done. Consider many ideas. Not all roads lead to Rome. This is just a useful guide to help you get started. I am a licensed contractor in the state of Maryland, a property manager, and an associate real estate broker who has worked in and around homes in almost every condition imaginable. I have seen it all in my career spanning over two decades. In the following chapters, I compiled a list to help you get started, along with points to consider after you sign on the dotted line. If you have already owned a home for a while, maybe there are a few tips here to help you too.

TEN IMPORTANT STEPS AFTER CLOSING

Step #1: *Change the locks and move in, in that exact order.* This is the most important thing a buyer should do after receiving their keys at closing. This is a particularly important step. I listed moving in and changing the locks as #1 because many properties may have been vacant for an extended period. This sometimes causes homes to be targets of vagrants or vandalism. Interior lights that are visible from the outside are an asset. It is important to make your presence known in the home, showing that the home is occupied, which lessens the probability of robberies or vandalism.

Some homes, such as bank foreclosures, frequently have preservation companies managing them. Sometimes there are delays in communication between banking institutions and their partners. Often, the preservation companies or field representatives may not be immediately aware that you have purchased the home. They may not receive instructions to cease management activities promptly. This is not done purposely or with ill intent, but as a result, they may continue to manage a property after closing. They commonly schedule maintenance dates in advance, and a few days of processing are required for them to be notified to cease management activities. Part of their job is to confirm that trespassers have not compromised the homes they manage. This is done by inspecting the inside. Many of the "key-alike" systems used on these homes are code-specific, and multiple entities have access to these properties. It is best to protect your family and assets by *immediately* changing the locks.

Step #2: *Transfer all the utilities into your name.* If you can schedule this before closing, do so. This will prevent disputes that may later arise regarding bills. Your agent can help you find utility companies in your area and provide contact phone numbers and billing addresses. There may be many companies that offer similar services, so it would be good to shop around. For example, there might be three or four Internet providers that provide services to a specific community. Research a few companies before closing to compare pricing and services that best suit your needs.

Step #3: *Visit your local department of motor vehicles and change the address on your driver's license to reflect your new address.* This step could also be important regarding real property taxes. Some jurisdictions require proof that you are occupying a home to award exemptions or real property tax discounts. Some state and local county jurisdictions also offer incentives for senior citizens, disabled individuals, veterans, and others. Please check with your local state of real property tax offices for information.

Step #4: *Immediately install or test existing smoke and carbon monoxide detectors* to ensure proper operation. Installing a burglar alarm may also be a good idea. Homeowner insurance companies may offer discounts for properties with security alarms and other protective devices installed.

Your agent is an important resource throughout this process. Ask for assistance with finding local companies, and do not be afraid to ask for referrals.

Step #5: *Understand how to pay your mortgage.* Most people pay for their homes by obtaining a mortgage or "deed of trust" on their property. This means you must pay monthly until the mortgage is paid in full. When you close, you may not get a coupon book or receive a bill. Be certain to reach out to your mortgagor within 30 days of closing to be sure you know your specific payment dates and different methods of payment. You may have the option of making payments online, by mail, at your local banking center, by phone, text, and so forth. Please communicate and become familiar with your mortgage company and payment methods so that you are not late and do not incur a late fee. At some point, your mortgage could be sold to a new loan servicer. Be careful not to make payments to a new servicer unless you receive documentation from your current servicer and the new servicer. To confirm this change is valid, call your mortgage servicer using the initial contact number issued to you at closing for verification before making payments to a different company. Some fraudulent entities and scammers have mailed letters to homeowners, instructing them that their mortgage company has changed. They may request homeowners to send their payments to them or call a different number to make payments. Be careful of these scams. They may even send correspondence using your actual servicer's name but with a different phone number or address. You may think you are paying your mortgage company when, in fact, you are paying a scammer.

Always verify any changes regarding your mortgage company by contacting them using the original, legitimate contact information you received when you originally purchased the home.

Step #6: *Contact your local post office and have your mailbox rekeyed, if necessary.* If you have a cluster mailbox, such as those in a townhome or condominium subdivision, *visit the local United States Postal Service to have the box rekeyed*. The seller of the home should have delivered a mailbox key to you at closing, if available. If the seller could not provide the local postal branch's location that services your home, search the Internet for your local Post Office by inputting your zip code + "post office" in the search engine. Call ahead to confirm that they service your address. You will need to provide a copy of your settlement/closing documents and a driver's license in some jurisdictions. Notify the post office that you are moving in by filling out a move-in card. Also, contact your creditors and other companies that you do business with regarding your address change. When vacationing or taking an extended trip away from home, you can request your mail be held at the post office until you return so that you don't run the risk of mail accumulating in the box, potentially alerting strangers that you are not home. The USPS gives you the option of scheduling a date you'd like them to start re-delivering, or you can have them hold the items until you visit their branch to pick up the mail. Please ask the United States Postal Service for details.

Step #7: *Clearly mark your house number on your house or mailbox in case of an emergency.* This could save precious time if emergency services, such as an ambulance, police, or fire department, need to find you. This step is especially important in rural areas where house numbers are not always in numerical order.

Step #8: *Buy one or more fire extinguishers.* Certainly, keep one in your kitchen. If you have a fireplace, keep another in a nearby closet. Leave them in the same location so you and your family are familiar with where they are located and practice using the extinguishers. This way, in case of a fire or emergency, you will know exactly where to go to retrieve it and what to do. In case of a fire, you may panic, and there will be no time to look for the units or read instructions. You can purchase fire extinguishers at most hardware stores. Fire extinguishers contain chemicals suited for different types of fires. Learn what they mean. Did you know that spraying a deep fryer fire with a Class A extinguisher could cause an explosion? Read the labels on the extinguishers to familiarize yourself and your family with the different classes and their respective uses.[1]

Type/Class/Usage:

> A: Solid materials that create ashes such as wood, paper, cloth, and plastic
>
> B: Flammable and combustible liquids such as gas, kerosene, alcohol, and grease
>
> C: Flammable gases such as propane, butane, and methane

D: Metals such as magnesium, potassium, aluminum, and titanium

CO_2 or E: Electrical or dry chemical fires; surge protectors, and outlets

F: Deep oil/fat fryers

K: Kitchen fires, grease, vegetable, and animal fats: not for use on deep fryers. See Class F above.

APW/Water: Only efficient for Class A items above.

Purchase the largest available extinguisher so it does not run out in the event of an emergency. Extinguishers expire over time and may leak. Do a periodic visual and mechanical inspection of your extinguisher's gauge to determine if a new one is needed, even if you have never used it. Do not make the mistake of needing to use it when there is a fire only to discover it is empty. Develop a plan with your family on what to do in case of a fire, noting exit windows and doors. Planning is not a cliché. Determine a place to meet with your family, in advance, in case of a fire so you can be certain everyone is safe. I suggested in step #7 to clearly mark your address on your mailbox or entrance so the fire department can locate your home in case of an emergency.

Tip: Never attempt to throw water or flour on a grease fire. This could potentially cause the fire to spread or ignite.

Step #9: *Purchase a fireproof or fire-resistant safe.* If the safe cannot be drilled or bolted to the floor or wall, hide or secure it in an inconspicuous place. In the event of a fire, fire-resistant and fireproof safes can protect passports, birth certificates, car titles, proof of insurance, important photos, and other important original documents that could be difficult or impossible to replace. Choose a location elevated from the basement. This safe should keep everything at your fingertips. This way, you will not have to think twice to remember where your important documents are if you must act quickly. This would help in an unfortunate case of a fire, flood, or natural disaster. Fire-resistant units take longer to burn, perhaps enough time to be saved, if a fire is extinguished promptly. There are also water-resistant safes. Consider a safe deposit box at a bank if a safe at home is not an option for you.

Step #10: *Save money for a "rainy day."* Although this is the last step on the list, it is particularly important and often the most overlooked precaution. In recent years, there have been cases of natural disasters, wildfires, furloughs, and a rare health epidemic where thousands of jobs have been lost. Multiple businesses closed indefinitely and permanently. In America and abroad, thousands of people were forced into unemployment. Many homeowners did not save for this "rainy day" and are still struggling to regain personal, household, and professional finances. This health crisis forced many to take time off work because of illness and caused the death of major wage earners within the household and other disadvantages, leaving many with no savings to pay rent or mortgage. This "rainy day" fund should also include funds to cover repairs for items that are not covered by your homeowner's insurance or warranty. It is best to save at least one year to 18 months of your monthly income for your emergency fund. Utility bill expenses can bounce around, and over time real estate taxes and other expenses, such as insurance, increase. Being prepared is always a great idea.

WARRANTY VS. HOMEOWNER INSURANCE

The best way to describe the differences between a warranty and homeowner insurance is to know homeowner insurance policies cover incidents that *could* happen, and warranties cover situations that *will* happen. Warranties for homes function similarly to a car warranty, allowing warranty holders to pay a deductible to have a service professional assess and, if covered, repair issues related to the items included in your policy. If you purchased a warranty before closing or at closing, or if a seller included one as an incentive to you, familiarize yourself with the benefits of your coverage.

Warranty policies can be tailored to suit specific needs, and not all policies are alike. Basic policies may lack coverage on some appliances or major functioning systems in a home. Some items, such as spas, hot tubs, pools, well pumps, and septic systems, require additional coverage. Be sure to understand the rules of your coverage so you can be prepared when you need to use it. Get clarification from the warranty company, if necessary. Keep the phone number of the warranty company and policy number in a prominent place if you need to call in an emergency.

Scenario: Your hot water begins to run cold. You call the warranty company and explain the issue, and if the water heater is a covered appliance, the company will schedule an appointment. Once they arrive, you would pay a deductible of approximately $75 for an assessment and repair. In some instances, if they cannot repair the appliance, they may replace it. A $75 deductible is much more affordable than the cost of a plumber and could help save money if you need something to be replaced, such as a new water heater. The service personnel contracted with warranty companies are normally reputable companies. Typically, they are *licensed and insured* plumbers and electricians, etc. This also helps prevent you from having to search for a contractor or handyman.

Tip: If you wait to purchase a warranty *after* closing, there may be a waiting period before you can make a claim. Buying the warranty at or before closing is a wise idea.

Homeowner insurance policies serve different purposes in contrast to warranties. Homeowner insurance policies are designed to protect the property for all parties with interest in the home and land, meaning the improvements, including the land of the property. These policies are designed to protect your home from peril. Peril is your exposure to risk or something that causes loss or destruction. Your home-inspection discoveries can cause you to inherit policy claim issues. Items reported in an inspection may be considered pre-existing conditions. These may cause a claim rejection because you were already aware that the concerns existed and are most likely responsible for curing those items at your policy's issuance. To be sure, ask your insurance agent.

Here are a few examples of perils: fires, hurricanes, tornadoes, and other natural disasters such as falling trees. These policies customarily combine various personal insurance protections, which can include losses occurring to one's home, its contents, loss of use (additional living expenses), or loss of other personal possessions of the homeowner, as well as liability insurance for accidents that may happen at home or at the hands of the homeowner within the policy territory.

It is your responsibility as a homeowner to keep your home safe and healthy for all who enter your premises. The premises include the exterior porch and yard. You could be held liable for things that happen on your lot or inside your home due to negligence or for not exhibiting due diligence. Sure, your Labrador retriever may be a calm dog, but if he gets excited and knocks someone down, causing an injury, you could be the target of a lawsuit. The same goes for other possible instances that could happen at your home that may seem harmless to many. Other examples include feeding someone food they may be allergic to, an accidental trip or fall, a dog or human falling into your pool, and the list goes on. The conclusion here is always to monitor your home and what happens there. Even though the actions in these scenarios may not be intentional or deliberate, if proper care is not taken to prevent these mishaps, homeowners could be considered negligent, and the result would be major claims against your insurance policy. Claims may cause your premium to be raised or canceled.

Become familiar with your policy and coverage. If your deductible is more expensive than the repair, consider paying a contractor to repair the damage instead of contacting your insurance company. Suppose you contact your insurance company to report damage, regardless of whether they will pay out a claim. In that case, they may require a repair to be completed and documented for their records within a short period to prevent the cancellation of your policy. There are time limitations to report claims. Make every effort to report covered damages quickly, unless you intend on repairing any damage yourself.

If your home is affected by moisture, such as a wet basement, it is smart to contact your insurance company to make a claim. Claims due to war, floods, earthquakes, sinkholes, nuclear explosions, and termites are typically excluded from coverage. Flood insurance can be purchased separately. Flood insurance normally covers water damage that occurs from the exterior of the home. If you experience moisture inside the home from other sources, your policy may cover the claim. Your covered items are outlined in the declarations and riders, if any, of your policy.

If you purchased a *multi-line policy*, the policy might include property insurance and liability coverage with a single premium for all risks. The premiums charged for these individual policies vary based on several factors. Some factors affecting premium price include proximity to a fire station, zip code areas, burglar alarms or security systems, interior sprinkler systems, and storm shelter precautions. Be sure to ask how you can qualify for discounts. Insurance companies would be happy to discuss them with you.

Homeowner insurance companies can offer discounts for bundling. Consider using the same company for your car, home, and other insurance needs. These policies do not normally cover appliances, so it is also smart to purchase a home warranty. Avoid policies with percentage deductibles. Instead, opt for a dollar-figure deductible or a percentage on claims. For example, a $500 deductible is much cheaper in most instances than a 1% charge deductible. The percentage charge deductible is calculated and charged on your home's total value, not the cost of repairs. Ask for a declaration page, including all riders, if applicable, so you can read your policy and become familiar with it.

Tip: Take date-stamped photos of your valuables to document what you own in case of a loss. Store the photos in the fire retardant safe suggested in step #9. You may need to provide these pictures with an insurance claim.

Double Tip: The homeowner insurance coverage on your home may cover your college students' items in their dorms while away at school, so you may not be required to buy a separate renter's policy to cover their computers, TVs, and other items. Did you know that personal property stolen from your car may also be covered on your homeowner insurance *instead* of your car insurance? Be sure to ask!

Triple Tip: Some people frequently entertain or have parties at their home with unusual entertainment such as electrical bulls, moon bounces, zip lines, carnival rides, and ponies. Although the activities may seem harmless, there may be a liability on your part if someone gets hurt in your home or on your land while engaging in these activities. A claim could be made against you that ccould become a major financial burden. Contact your insurance company and inquire if incidents are covered. If they are not covered in your policy, consider having guests sign waivers of liability before engaging in specific activities. Do not feel shy about requesting this. Many public places require patrons to sign these documents, so why shouldn't you? You can get waiver forms online or have an attorney draft one for you.

HOMEOWNER ASSOCIATION, CONDO, AND FRONT-FOOT BENEFIT FEES

Homeowner fees and condominium association fees are similar in some ways and contrast in more. A condominium purchase is different from purchasing a home or structure subject to a Homeowner Association's rules. Purchasing a condo is purchasing a specific type of ownership, in contrast, for example, purchasing a cooperative or a "coop." Purchasing real estate is similar to these ownership types because you normally have the opportunity and privilege to review the rules, bylaws, covenants, and restrictions that could affect your ownership *before* you close on your purchase. Note that purchasing a coop is not purchasing a physical structure. If you bought a coop, that means you bought shares in the cooperative corporation which owns the building where the physical structure you want to occupy is located. You now own an allocated number of shares that depends upon the size and location of the unit. At closing, instead of receiving a deed, you receive a stock certificate and a lease or occupancy agreement. As a shareholder, you have become part-owner of the entire building with a proprietary lease for a specific unit only.

If you purchased a condominium, your real estate agent or title company probably explained that condominium ownership is a type of ownership, not a style of home. There is a common misconception that a condo is a one-level, apartment-style home. However, condos can have two, three, four, or more levels. With this type of ownership, you own everything *in* your unit on your side of the walls. You only own a title to the unit and not the land beneath the unit or building. With the other owners, you now share the title to common areas such as tot lots, parking lots, pools, lobbies, and other amenities.

Some bylaws and restrictions must be followed to avoid fines and penalties. Be certain to thoroughly read these documents to understand the processes involved, especially if you wish to modify your unit. A boundary survey may be required after you purchase if you desire to make exterior modifications to your home, such as having a shed installed, driveway extended, or a fence erected. Getting a boundary survey before you purchase is not required. It is an extra expense but is necessary to prove you are not encroaching on someone else's yard or lot.

It is important to know what your coop, condo, or Homeowner Association (HOA) fees include. For example, in some communities, if you become delinquent on your community fees, you could lose your right to a designated parking space or worse. Your credit could also be affected by a personal judgment or other collection activities because of unpaid HOA fees. Be certain to learn how many homeowner or neighborhood associations are involved in governing your community. Often, there is more than one per community, and fees may be simultaneously mandatory for both. Read the bylaws for all governing groups and stay up to date on changes and updates. You will need to provide these rules to a buyer if you decide to sell your home.

You would also need to pass these documents to all tenants should you decide to rent your property. A revised copy would be necessary to ensure current and accurate information.

Tip: Arrears on condo fees can result in foreclosure in certain areas, also known as "super lien" states. Please be aware of the regulations in your area. The possible consequences were most likely explained in your disclosures prior to closing, and there may have been a document for you to sign to acknowledge receipt of those disclosures. Check your deed for an applicable covenant or rider.

Double Tip: If you rent your property to tenants, do not forget to present a copy of any bylaws, covenants, and restrictions before executing the lease. You do not want to be responsible and face possible fines resulting from not properly notifying tenants of the rules they must follow while they reside in the community.

Front-Foot Benefit Fees

Front-foot benefit fees (also known as deferred water sewer charges) are costs, or capital expense fees, charged to an owner to offset fees incurred to install and connect existing city plumbing lines to a newly built home. Instead of paying the municipality a single large fee to hook up lines to a new home or new community, the utility company spreads the fee over several years to the homeowner as annual assessments. This can be used as a conversion process for existing homes to convert a well to public water usage also. This cost is transferred from one homeowner to another as the house is sold or conveyed until the end of the term. This fee is not associated with water and sewer usage. This fee is another example of a "material fact" discussed in the introduction of this book. The seller or agent should disclose front-foot benefit fees before the execution of your sales contract. These fees and any arrears owed by the seller are commonly discovered during a title search before closing. A declaration of water and sewer charges should be recorded in public records, and the title company most likely disclosed them upon their title search before you closed on your home. These fees are charged separately by government entities and often by privately-owned or managed companies. If delinquent, these fees frequently become liens or tax fees that may attach to the property or a personal judgment against you, which could harm your credit. In these cases, the property cannot be sold until the arrears are paid. The fees would be deducted from your net bottom line, if any, at closing. Delinquencies normally carry hefty interest fees and penalties that could easily and quickly eat up your equity.

CALL BEFORE YOU DIG

Have you ever wondered why some areas have total blackouts or plumbing is shut down for hours because of the main waste line or sewer line damage? In some instances, those underground lines were disturbed, unknowingly, by someone digging where they should not have been digging. There are many things installed underground that you may not realize. Some of those underground utilities are connected to your home, and others are likely connected to your whole community. Before digging and installing poles or stakes into the ground on the exterior of a property, you should call the Common Ground Alliance, where they will provide information for your state-specific underground utility organization. These organizations will come to your home to assess the area you plan to dig and often will mark underground utility lines to avoid. This ensures that you are not planning to dig where there are underground storage tanks, gas lines, electric wires, utility cables, plumbing, septic drain field lines, or other pipes. Even something as seemingly harmless as installing a mailbox has the potential to cause problems. The phone number for this service can be obtained from your county or city's community resource services, or you can call 8-1-1. Most areas offer Miss Utility services free of charge, while others charge a very nominal fee. Digging without an assessment could interrupt service in an entire town. Worse, digging without an assessment could potentially cost you your life. So, call before you dig!

PLUMBING

Plumbing systems are one of the most frequently repaired items in a home. Most plumbing repairs are small and could be repaired without the help of a plumber. For example, a leaky sink trap or running toilet is not considered a major plumbing repair. If you have a leaking tub or pipe, hire a professional. Some plumbing repairs can be fixed quickly just by tightening a washer or joint screw. A new flush valve in a toilet could be a do-it-yourself project that will save you approximately $100 or more. If you are not familiar with these items, do not try to fix them. Call a professional.

It is common for tree roots to puncture plumbing lines and clog drains. These repairs are more difficult to diagnose and fix. If you live in a municipality with a serviced water company, learn who is responsible for necessary repairs to outdoor waste lines. Research and obtain documented explanations defining boundaries to learn who pays for repairs on the street and the plumbing line from the street to the house. Ask the water company if they offer a warranty or a special insurance plan to cover water line damage or possible liability *before* an incident occurs.

Consider installing a water leak detector, a flood protection system, or a point-of-use water detection system to prevent major interior flooding. These systems protect your home from water damage caused by faulty or leaky appliances and pipes. When installed, these units can help to prevent major moisture catastrophes. They are regulated by sensors designed to shut down the affected water line, close the valve, and set off an alarm if an issue strikes. This could prevent a minor leak from becoming a major flood.

If you plan to leave your home for an extended period, it is a good idea to "plumberize" it. I created this term to describe different things you can do to save your plumbing system from disasters when you are not home. It has a similar definition to the term "winterize." If you depart in the summer, lower the temperature on your water heater to prevent the pressure from building up and bursting the plumbing lines at the water heater. You could also disable the hot water. If you live in an area with severely cold winters, you should drain and turn off outside water spigots or other drains to prevent the pipes from bursting. If you have unfinished areas of a basement with exposed plumbing pipes, please insulate the pipes with foam or other specialized plumbing insulation. Turn off external water hose bibs and internal spigots and drain the pipes on the outside by turning them on. Covering outside hose bibs with insulated bib covers could also help to protect those lines. Consider leaving a heating source active within the home.

If it is impossible to leave a heating source active, have the home winterized until you return. "Winterizing" includes draining your water heater of all water. This will eliminate moisture from the pipes, removing the probability of water freezing in the pipes and causing damage. Keep crawl space doors closed and insulated to prevent freezing temperatures from affecting well-water tanks and lines or other components under your home. Gutters also need to be maintained in the winter months to prevent moisture infiltration. Take note – you should turn off the power to the water heater before draining it. Keeping the power on your electric water heater tank while it is empty could cause damage. Tankless hot water systems are designed with heat exchanger systems and should also be winterized during the cold season, if necessary.

Tip: Qualified agents and property managers are good resources to consult to help maintain your home, should you anticipate an extended period of absence from your property. Always protect your investment!

Double Tip: Slow draining pipes are not always a result of clogged waste lines. Clogged roof air vents could be the culprit. The vent could be clogged with bird nests, leaves, or debris.

WHAT IS A GRINDER PUMP?

If your home is in a low-lying area or ravine, the architect or builder who drew plans for your home probably included a grinder pump. Grinder pumps are commonly confused with sump pumps because of their visual appearance, but the two differ in purpose. I discuss sump pumps in a different chapter. Although grinder pumps are normally located on the home's exterior, they are part of a home's waste-plumbing system and can be on a home's interior. The grinder pump operates by pumping waste line water up a hilly area or incline into a sump pump, city water waste line, or septic tank.

Simply put, a grinder pump assists with defying gravity. This system normally needs power to operate. Most likely, there is a breaker or fuse inside your home or shed to facilitate this. In the event of a power outage, this system may become inoperable.

Installation of a grinder pump often requires a permit. Your local municipality should have blueprints on record if you need to locate the pump, showing the locale of your grinder pump on your lot from the installation permits. Contact your local office of building permits for more information on the age, location, and other details regarding your grinder pump.

WELL AND SEPTIC

Homes require different types of maintenance, depending upon the location. Homes in rural areas, meaning homes in less populated, heavily wooded areas, require unique maintenance forms compared to urban, suburban, and water-oriented communities. Homes are designed to use different types of systems depending on their environment. Most homes in suburban and urban areas have public or county utilities for water and waste. Homes in water-oriented communities or rural areas are more likely to have well water and septic-waste systems. Some homes in water-oriented communities may also be built on stilts with their exterior systems, such as heat pumps, elevated from the ground, to prevent water intrusion from frequent flooding or high tides. This depends, of course, on the distance to the nearest body of water or the frequency of past intrusions upon the area. Many different sources can cause moisture infiltration.

If your home includes well water or a septic-waste system, there are important precautionary measures to maintain these systems to prevent problems. With a well water system, you may want to perform a water quality test at least once every two years to be certain your water is safe. After a well repair, the system should be decontaminated to rid any contaminants that could have entered the well during the repair. Some area regulations mandate that well repair professionals perform decontaminations as a part of the repair. Actions involving the repair and handling of wells, well maintenance, and well water purification are regulated by environmental agencies that govern each jurisdiction. Although the EPA's Water Protection Act only covers public drinking water systems, most states regulate private household wells through local health departments, and most have limited rules. For example, in some areas, licensed well companies cannot hold a septic repair license simultaneously. I believe the reason for this is to make sure the septic person is not using the same tools to clean your septic tank for repairing your well. Whatever the reason, that prohibition sounds great to me! Some mortgage loan products require a water quality test to be performed, documenting that the water is safe before a buyer can close on a home.

City water or public water, serviced by a municipality, is normally wastewater, cleaned through a filtration process, and then redistributed to you at a cost from a cleaning reservoir at a facility. Well water is natural water or groundwater from rain, springs, and other natural sources instead of city water or public water. The EPA hosts a website with a "Consumer Confidence Report"[2] designed to help you find out where your water comes from and what's in it.

Excessive browning in your toilets and sinks with well water could indicate you have hard water. Most likely, there is mineral, metal, or rust build-up/sediment in your water. Excessive sediment in water supplied by a well could also indicate that a steel-well casing is deteriorating. Purchasing an inexpensive water softener could help resolve your worries with a hard water concern. However, a deteriorating well casing will need to be evaluated by a well water professional. Most water filtration systems use natural softeners or salt to filter water. There are many different systems on the market, including those that do not use electricity to run. Many biological contaminants potentially live in well water. This could mean that washing your hands could be making your hands dirtier instead of cleaner! Ask your doctor if you are immunocompromised as you may need to boil well water before drinking it. Test strips and water meters to measure contaminants, alkalinity, pH balance, or pollutants in your water can be purchased online or at hardware stores.

Most well water systems include a well water pump. Parts of a well water system deteriorate over time and may need to be replaced. A well water system normally requires electric power to run properly. If you have a leak in your home or leave your water running, remember that your well pump is also running and utilizing power. Excessive use of your well pump from plumbing leaks or similar issues can lessen the lifespan of your well pump. You do not have a water bill with well water, but you most likely receive an electric bill.

Install a backup power system to ensure you can continue to use these systems in case of a power outage. Otherwise, if your power goes out, you will not be able to flush toilets, take showers, wash dishes, and so forth. Backup power systems, or generators, can be found at your local hardware store. Some of the systems utilize marine batteries, and power packs can also be purchased. These remain plugged in during normal usage, and they run for approximately 24 hours after a power outage. If your power is out for an extended period, it may be necessary to have the pressure of your well pump tube re-engaged or calibrated.

How does a well water system work?

Old wells were built differently than how they are built today. Older wells were built approximately four-feet wide, on average, but with vastly different types of materials than those used today. Older wells were frequently built with brick or rock walls and with manual pumps at the top or a bucket on a crank connected to a rope.

Some homes still utilize a variation of the older units but with a few modifications. Most modern-day wells are built with steel or PVC wells, about four inches wide. This is a far cry from the old, average, four-foot-wide wells. Wells have evolved to be smaller and more efficient, but they require special tools and equipment to repair. PVC is now thought to be more efficient than steel well casings because of water's eventual effect on metal over time. Even if galvanized, water causes steel to erode. Most well drillers are phasing out of the installation of new steel wells.

In my opinion, residential wells are a lot less sophisticated than I imagined they would be by now. Modern wells have electric pumps at the end of a hose connected to your home and plumbing. Shallow wells may have the pump above ground. The repairs of deep wells with long hoses most likely include submersible pumps. They require heavy equipment or several individuals to handle the simplest repair. The phrase, "you never miss your water until your well runs dry," will never have more meaning than if you ever need a well repair at your home. There are temporary water stations that can be installed at your home if you are out of water for an extended period during a repair. Call your local health department for resources on well water testing labs in your area.

Your well casing may have a tag secured to it with a registration number and other identifying information regarding your well's installation date or installer. Contact the permits office if a tag is not available on your casing. The information the tag reveals about your well's history can be extremely helpful if you need a repair.

Your septic system is your waste management system. This type of system prevents you from having a waste management fee. Public waste management is an expense. Many people are unaware that in some communities with water and sewer fees, it costs to flush toilets and pour water down the drain. This is true! A septic waste system saves you money in this regard. A private septic system is normally located underground in your yard. Some people share a septic tank with a few homes nearby. This is called a shared septic system.

How does a septic system work?

Your septic tank is constantly working for you. Your waste is funneled out to this system through a drain field and into a tank underground.

The tanks are normally concrete, polyethylene, or fiberglass, covered by layers of soil that assist with its operation and a drain field or leach fields/leach drains, which help remove filter contaminants and impurities from the liquid that could emerge from the septic tank. The tank holds the wastewater long enough to allow solids to settle to the bottom, forming sludge, while the oil and grease float to the top as scum. An outlet prevents the sludge and scum from leaving the tank and traveling into the drain field area. The liquid wastewater then exits the tank into the drain field.

If the drain field is overloaded with too much liquid, it may flood, causing sewage to flow to the ground, surface, or create backups in toilets and sinks. If it is overloaded by too much solid waste, this increases the risk of a clogged drain field and possibly a complete septic backup or breakdown. Lastly, the wastewater percolates into the soil, naturally removing harmful bacteria, viruses, and nutrients. A septic system needs to be pumped at least every three to five years. If your system suffers recurring drain field failure, has extremely permeable (or impermeable) soil, a high-water table, or other specific wastewater penetration issues, a mound system installation may be an alternative to the traditional drain field (*see Image B*).

Monitor what is poured into sinks and flushed through toilets into a septic system. Even some items that are labeled flushable may not be safe. Items used in your system should be labeled *"biodegradable"* or *"safe for septic systems."* Non-biodegradable solids that are not broken down or dissolved in your septic system have the potential to cause major problems and necessary repairs. The more solid, non-biodegradable materials you flush, the more frequently you will need your system to be pumped. There are products on the market that assist with breaking down the solids in your system. Long-term neglect has the potential to cause thousands of dollars of needed repairs to a septic system.

How do I know if my well system is failing?

If your well-pump system is failing, you will most likely experience at least one of the following:

- Low water pressure at your faucets or spigots
- No water
- Cloudy water or sediment in the water
- Loud noises from the pumps or faucets
- Air spitting from the faucets
- Breaker tripping or power outages
- High electric bills from an overactive pressure tank or pump or the system turns on when not in use.

If you begin to smell an odor only when running the hot water, do not assume that the smell always indicates contaminated water. If the hot water emits an odor, you may have an issue with your water heater. Call a plumber.

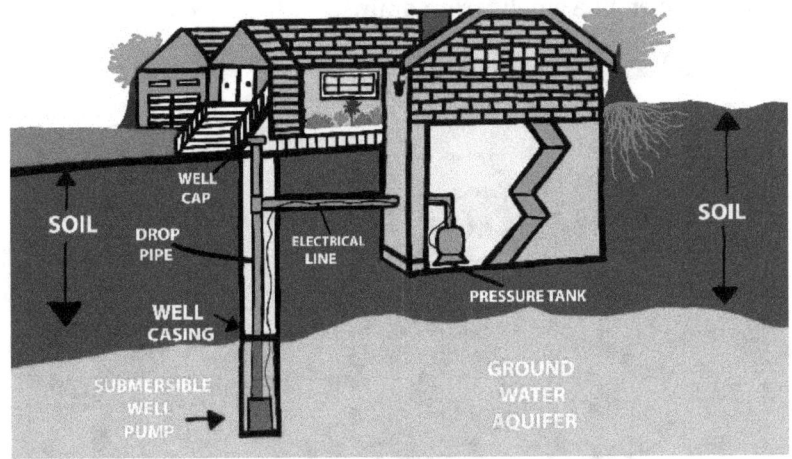

Image A

How do I know if my septic system is failing?

If your septic system is failing, you will most likely experience at least one of the following issues:

- A strong odor around the septic tank and drain field area
- Bright green, spongy grass on the drain field, even during dry weather
- Wastewater backing up into household drains on the inside of the house

- Pooling water or muddy soil around your septic system or in your basement
- Difficulty flushing toilets
- Foul, sewer-like smells from drains.

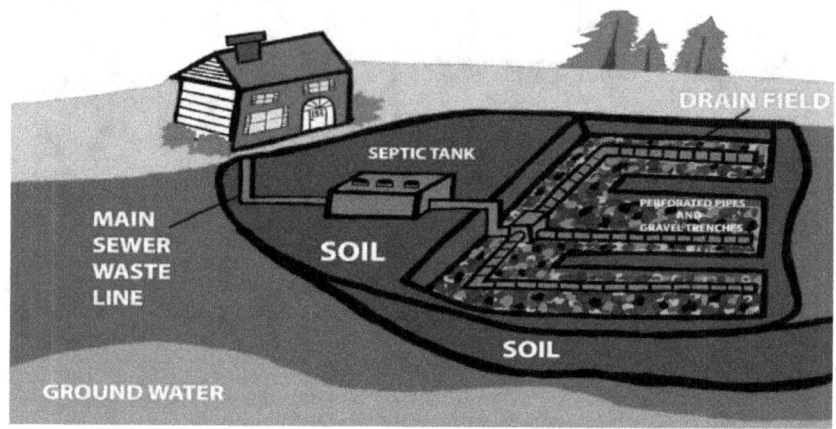

Image B

ROOF AND GUTTERS

Many homeowners have expressed that they were unaware that lack of maintenance to gutters and roofs could result in moisture infiltration leading to a flooded basement or, worse, *mold*. Most roofs are designed to lead water into the gutters, down a downspout, and away from a home's foundation and base. If any of these mechanisms are defective, lack maintenance, or need repair, your home becomes vulnerable to moisture infiltration. Keep the gutter clean and free of falling leaves or debris. Watch for loose nails, buckled shingles on the eaves, and other defects, and you should have minimal moisture problems for the full life span of your roof. Some window frame leaks are a result of roof issues. Keep in mind that if you own an attached home, such as a townhome, duplex, or apartment-style condo. If your neighbor has a leak or neglects their property, it could also affect your home. If you have a condo or homeowner association, be certain to read the documents associated with your community to interpret and understand who will be responsible for those repairs. *Your* leak could damage a neighboring property causing you to foot the bill for a repair. Call a local handyman, contractor, or roofer if you are unsure of the cause of leaks.

If your home has a basement with a stairwell entry/exit, there should be a drain at the bottom of the stairwell to divert water from the door, preventing it from entering. It is imperative to keep this drain free of trash, debris, leaves, and any other article that could prevent proper operation. Install a screen or grate to prevent leaves and other debris from clogging the drain.

Most tasks involving roofs and gutters require the use of a ladder. If you are not physically able to use a ladder, please employ the services of a professional. Do not take a chance of falling. The ANSI states, "There are more than 300 ladder-related deaths and over 130,000 emergency room visits related to ladders each year, as well as 2,000 ladder-related injuries every day."[3]

Tip: When purchasing a ladder, be sure to purchase the appropriate ladder for your weight capacity. There are color codes and types to help you choose the correct ladder. Most ladders are labeled with a weight class and type. If you need help, ask a sales associate at the hardware store.

GRADING

When doing a seasonal check of your home, grading is an important part to inspect. Grading is the deciding factor for which way stormwater and rain will flow at your foundation. Evaluating whether your grading is *positive* or *negative* is key. *Positive* grading is good because it means your grading slopes down, away from your home, and leads water in that direction. *Negative* grading is a slope leading toward your house, causing water to flow into your foundation. Maintain proper grading around the perimeter of your home to assist with creating a runoff. Create and maintain a slight slope at your foundation to help water runoff and away from the foundation instead of a 90º degree angle between the foundation and the ground.

Trees should not be planted or allowed to grow close to your home's foundation. Roots underneath the ground can grow into your foundation, causing cracks and issues that could be costly to repair. If you feel compelled to plant trees close to home because of neighbors' proximity, consider installing a root or planting bar to prevent the root from growing too close to the home's foundation. Consider installing a planting bar on your lot to protect your foundation if your neighbor plants a tree or shrubbery close to your foundation. This will help keep *their* plant or tree from damaging your home.

FOUNDATION OR SETTLEMENT CRACKS

Settlement is a physiological act of nature, and there is nothing mankind can do about it. Do your own science project, and stick something, anything, halfway under the ground and let it sit. After some time, the item you stuck into the ground will be affected by the elements of moisture, erosion, heat, cold, and wind; you name it. Gravity and science have their way! With the very same concept in mind, understand that most homes are built into a dirt foundation with a combination of natural and man-made materials. Over time, outside variables affect the stability of your home and its foundation. There could be earthquakes, hurricanes, and tornados. On the less traumatic scale, there could be a lot of rain or simply age and time. Settlement is the reaction of dirt moving under your home as it settles into the dirt beneath. Natural settlement is the reason a newly constructed home shows signs of nail pops and seam gaps. Many cracks do not require repairs, but some do. One rule of thumb for cracks that I have learned over the year is to measure a crack, and if it is a centimeter wide or less, it is considered less than serious, but it is always better to veer on the side of caution.

As I stated before, prevention is better than cure. Big cracks normally begin as smaller cracks that eventually widen. Cement fillers can often repair small hairline cracks if they are not indicative of structural damage. It is best to examine your house at the beginning of the fall to determine if repairs need to be made, so the cracks do not worsen over the winter months. Cracks expand in cold weather. The thin crack you saw in August could become a wide, gaping crack if not repaired before ice and rain penetrate, harden, and widen the gap. This could also widen the problem *and* the potential for a costly repair. Major cracks or structural issues can be costly and should be evaluated by an inspector or structural engineer to determine their severity.

What is radon, and how does it affect me?

Radon is a naturally occurring radioactive gas produced by uranium breakdown in soil, rock, and water. Radon affects homes by entering through the foundation or basement and is very rarely present in well water. If it is in the water, it could be released into the air when showering and other household water uses. The EPA states that radon is the leading cause of lung cancer for non-smokers and the second leading cause of lung cancer for the general population. A radon-reduction unit can be installed in homes. The EPA suggests that we should have our homes treated for radon if the levels are four picocuries per liter, pCi/L or higher.[4] Radon levels less than four pCi/L still pose a risk. Radon levels can change unexpectedly and can vary from house to house. It is possible to be affected by radon even if no other home in your community is affected. Because radon is a colorless, odorless gas, there is no way to tell if you have radon in your home unless you experience health issues. To be safe, I recommend having your home tested periodically, especially if you experience unexplained respiratory health concerns or if other homes in your community have been affected.

MOISTURE INFILTRATION AND DAMAGE

A few causes of moisture damage were mentioned in earlier chapters. It was important to first learn about the functionality of other parts of a house before discussing moisture infiltration sources in detail. One of the most frequently asked questions I receive is regarding moisture/water damage. Moisture is one of the most feared and potentially troublesome problems one can have as a homeowner. This is because its source is not always easily found, its causes are frequently improperly assessed, and its damage can be devastating.

Moisture, or mold, is a part of our natural environment and can be found everywhere. All moisture infiltration has a source or several sources simultaneously. Almost all can be cured by different measures of action and at different prices. Earlier, I explained that roof damage could cause moisture to infiltrate. This is true. I also explained that a lack of gutter maintenance could also cause a home to be vulnerable to water damage. This is also true. I mentioned that a lack of proper grading and structural cracks could also be culprits. All of this is true; however, these are not the *only* sources of moisture damage or water intrusion. Moisture infiltration could result from one of these issues, two simultaneously, or three to four at once.

There are many ways water can intrude into a home and cause damage. It is important to do your best to prevent and treat any causes.

Long-term moisture, open, exposed, or unseen, could attract mold, potentially aggravating allergies or cause other serious health risks. FEMA states:

"Mold growths, or colonies, can start to grow on a damp surface within 24-48 hours. They reproduce by spores" that travel to the air. "They can also produce mild to severe health problems".[5]

A few adverse health problems listed by FEMA include respiratory problems, skin irritations, and effects on the nervous system. I interpret this as an issue that could be dangerous and should be resolved quickly.

I have listed the potential causes of the moisture infiltration that could lead to discoloration or mold. You should consult a certified mold inspector and get a mold test if you suspect an issue to determine if there are contaminants in your home. This list offers some clues that you can use as a starting point if you suspect a moisture issue, but it should not be considered a complete list of all existing causes. Each case is unique, and your issue may not be listed here. This list will help you get started if you feel you have a small problem that you may repair on your own. Use it as a guide to explain your problem if you need to describe what you see to a contractor.

Some areas of discoloration may be easy to cure by cleaning and keeping areas dry, but some moisture may result in mold spore growth. Not all areas of discoloration contain mold. Some mold can be toxic and poisonous. Only a mold inspection, including obtaining a lab test with a sample collection, can determine if discoloration contains mold or the type of mold and toxicity level, if any. Regardless, you want to take steps to eradicate it in your home to prevent spreading.

Moisture damage could be a result of the following:

- Cracks in the foundation
- Lack of or defective window well covers
- Roof damage (including, but not limited to, missing shingles, damage to plywood sheathing sections, defective roof ridge vent, soffits, fascia, and bargeboard)
- Gutter damage or lack of gutter cleaning and maintenance
- Missing downspouts
- Missing downspout extensions
- Cracks in a porch (front, rear, or side)
- Lack of grading/improper grading
- Defective windows or window frames
- Siding damage or defects
- The home is situated at the bottom of a hill
- Defective sump pump or loss of power at the sump pump
- Improperly aligned roof venting
- A surge in extreme rain or inclement weather
- Ice damming at gutters
- Tree roots affecting the foundation

- Trees lifting shingles or weighing down gutters
- Plumbing leaks (could be inside the wall and visually obstructed from view)
- Busted pipes
- Washing machine leak
- Defective dishwasher
- Leaky sink trap or other plumbing leaks
- Unventilated bathrooms or crawl spaces
- Lack of air conditioning in an improperly ventilated home
- Defective or missing roof flashing
- Defective or damaged chimney flashing
- Improperly installed decks or patios
- Faulty grinder pumps (or lack of installation)
- Floods from neighboring bodies of water
- Not keeping exterior drains unclogged and clear of leaves and debris
- Chipped, peeling paint on exterior window frames and trim
- Lack of ventilation in a bathroom
- Tree roots too close to a home's foundation could compromise the structural integrity of a foundation underground
- Excessive stormwater runoff and storm floods
- The need to waterproof the foundation.

This long list includes only a few possibilities that could cause water infiltration into a home. Always have a licensed specialist assess damages to determine if your home needs repair.

Could your house be making you sick?

Do you or your family have allergies or mysterious health concerns that you have not been able to control or manage? Research the construction materials used to build your home. The results may surprise you. You may find that some homes, old and new, could be making you sick. Some people have allergic reactions to certain materials used to build, finish, or renovate the places they live or work. This could attribute directly to specific airborne building contaminants. Chemical or combustion pollutants, building construction materials, heavy metals, biological pollutants, among other things, could be possible sources of allergic reactions or irritations to human health. Many common household products contain ingredients, some known as volatile organic compounds (VOCs). VOCs have been reported to contain chemicals that could aggravate asthma, allergies, and other conditions. Lead-based paint and animal hair plaster have long been under the scrutiny and intense research studies of many health organizations. Inadequate ventilation, dust mites, and moisture trapped inside your walls could be affecting your health. In the *Indoor Air Pollution, An Introduction for Health Professionals* report, the EPA states that carbon monoxide poisoning is often misdiagnosed as cold or flu because of the respiratory impact of pollutants from misuse malfunctioning combustion devices.[6]

Railroad ties are often used as decorative or functional lawn and garden edges. However, railroad ties are commonly treated with creosote, lead, and arsenic, or a combination of other chemicals such as chromium. These could seep into your soil, water supply, plants, and gardens. Exposure to dangerous radon levels, asbestos, carbon monoxide, and other airborne contaminants warrant a trip to the doctor if you have unexplained ailments, allergies, or other illnesses. It is always better to be safe than sorry.

WHAT IS A SUMP PUMP?

A sump pump is normally located in a small well at a low point of your home, most likely the basement. You may have more than one in your home. It is a pump designed to capture any water that settles in the well basin drawn by other lines connected to the waterproofing sump pump system. The sump pump then disperses the water out of the basin and away from the home's foundation.

A sump pump system operates similarly to the flush valve system in the back of standard toilets but in reverse. Once the water in your tank reaches a certain height in your toilet, the water stops to avoid overflowing. Once the water reaches a certain height in your sump pump, the system begins pumping the water out of the home, thus preventing it from overflowing in the sump pump well and into your home. Sump pumps operate on power. Rain and windstorms can frequently cause power outages, coincidentally when your sump pump is most needed. Periodically check your pump by pulling the valve. When you pull the pump's height valve towards you, the pump should cut on. If it does not, be sure it is plugged in and the breaker has not tripped. If you are still unsure, contact a handyman or handywoman.

Tip: Install a backup power system or battery to your sump pump. These can be purchased at your local hardware store. This way, if the power goes out in a storm, your sump pump will continue to work.

ELECTRICAL

If you bought an older home, your home's electrical system might not be prepared for all that the millennium has brought into your daily life. In the past, not many homes used halogen-recessed lighting. Now, in addition to multiple computers and appliances, larger homes, and high-capacity units, we use more electronics than ever. You may need an assessment of your home to be sure its electrical capacity supports your needs. An indication that you may need a modification of your electrical system, or *heavy up*, would be frequent tripping of your breakers when using several outlets at once. If multiple items go out at once, check your fuse or electrical panel to see if a breaker has tripped. Tripping is a safety feature of electrical panels with breakers. It signals the interruption of the current in your panel to one or more specific breakers. When this happens, the breaker trips to cut off the power flow through that breaker, thus preventing a power overload and a possible fire. It's also an indication that you are attempting to use too much power through that breaker from its source or more than its capacity is designed to distribute.

Be careful when opening and operating breakers. If your breakers are not labeled, you can look at the breakers to see which one has tripped. Breakers should be in the ON or OFF position. You can identify the tripped breaker by locating a circuit that has tripped to the middle. Turn the breaker to the OFF position and then back to the ON position. If the breaker gives an arching or sizzling sound, do not force it on. Turn the breaker back to the OFF position, and immediately contact a professional electrician. Electrical systems are partly designed to warn you if something is wrong. Please pay attention to what you hear, see, and smell regarding electrical systems.

I have heard a few inspectors instruct buyers to open a panel box and flip breakers with the right hand because it is furthest from the heart. I'm not sure if that would prevent physical harm, but it doesn't sound like a bad idea. A better idea is to hire a professional. If you plug in an appliance and see a spark, hear a sizzling sound, or see smoke, discontinue the use of that outlet and call an electrician. To avoid possible electrocution, never use electrical appliances near water. *Never* attempt to repair any electrical item on your own. This could be extremely dangerous and result in fire or death. Use a stud finder to locate electrical wires inside a wall before driving nails to hang pictures or securing furniture. This prevents damage to your electrical system and possible electrocution.

Tip: Never use extension cords with high-voltage appliances or items. Please read safety precautions that are included with your appliances, and *never* leave extension cords plugged in when sleeping, leaving home, or without constant supervision.

HEATING VENTILATION & AIR CONDITIONING (HVAC)

All heating and air conditioning units vary. Whether you have an oil furnace, boiler radiator system, gas forced air furnace, heat pump, or central air conditioning unit; they should all be serviced at least once a year. Change your furnace filters at the beginning of each season. If you have allergies, installing a HEPA filter more frequently than once a season could help. The higher the HEPA or MERV rating, the better.

Gas furnaces have manufacturer-mandated clearance requirements regarding the locale of the unit due to open flames on the system. Always provide clearance around the front of the unit to maintain a safe distance. If the unit is in a closet or enclosed area, a vented or louver door is recommended for ventilation purposes. This helps prevent gas buildup. Manufacturers have unique specifications for each unit based on its size. Consult them for assistance if you need help with your unit. You may need the model and the serial number of your unit to obtain this information.

Having your unit serviced can potentially catch small problems that could become big problems. Servicing can also keep your unit at optimal performance, preventing you from using a unit that may be burning more energy, thus causing higher energy bills. A small refrigerant leak caught at a service call could be covered by that service call's cost. Buying a new compressor when low refrigerant levels burn your current unit out could cost approximately $1,000 or more.

Changing filters may seem like a nuisance, but continuing to use dirty, clogged, and contaminated filters could put a strain on your heating system. Imagine the impact of an asthma attack on your airways. Consider your filter and filtration system in the lungs of your furnace. If air cannot flow freely through the filter, your motor will be strained to operate properly, and your system may fail as a result. Your baseboard heating systems are easier to maintain in this regard because there are no filters to change, but they should be kept clear of dust, debris, furniture, and other items. Furniture and drapes should be meticulously placed with a clearance to avoid fire hazards. Baseboard heating is used more frequently now in mobile and manufactured homes. The older units that are still available in homes should be checked for energy efficiency. If you have an issue with your furnace or heat pump, check the batteries in your thermostat. Your thermostat's display may include a feature that alerts you if the battery is low. After changing the batteries, wait five to ten minutes before turning on the unit. This will prevent possible damage to the relay.

Insert stoves, like wood-burning stoves, are fueled by several source materials. Some are wood burning, pellet, or gas-fueled hearth appliances. There are also electric stove inserts. You can install a blower on most inserts to improve heat distribution.

BOILER HEATING SYSTEMS

Older homes may contain boiler heating systems. These systems need to be serviced just like other HVAC systems. Boiler systems are typically fueled by water, but there are also oil-fired and gas-fired boiler systems. These systems should be properly maintained to continue to warm your home properly. These systems are desired and favored by homeowners who have limited access to natural gas systems. If you own a home with an oil-fired furnace older than ten years old, have a technician replace your nozzle. Older, outdated units are not as energy-efficient as the newer units, but they can be inexpensively modified. A smaller nozzle could save you as much as 10% on your fuel bill. This process is called de-rating. Adding a time delay to your water boiler system could also help you save on energy costs.

There are systems fueled by biodiesel, a cleaner-burning alternative to foreign petroleum. Biodiesel is diesel fuel. This fuel can contain vegetable oil, animal fat, recycled grease, or a formulation of all these substances with an alcohol ester. Some scientists claim that this fuel is safer, biodegradable, and produces fewer air pollutants than traditional diesel fuel.[7]

FLOORING

There are hundreds of types of flooring to choose from for your humble abode. The types available to choose from include hardwood, bamboo, natural or engineered wood, cork, vinyl, and many types of carpet, tile, marble, and stone. Many others exist, and the list goes on and on. Here are some things to consider if you plan to replace the flooring or need help caring for your existing floors:

1. Cost
2. Installation difficulty
3. Durability
4. Cleaning difficulty/cost to maintain.

When considering which type of flooring is best for your needs, consider those four factors. Start by making a chart and comparing each type. Consider how much traffic you have in your home to decide if you should opt for more durable flooring over less durable, hard-to-clean flooring. Consider sunlight that may beam on your floor and bleach the color. Note the moisture and temperature for your climate. Be practical when placing certain types of floor coverings. It may not be appropriate to place a carpet in the kitchen where spills are possible due to cooking, washing dishes, and so forth.

GENERAL MAINTENANCE

General maintenance on a home sounds like common sense that does not warrant defining. Most of that statement is true; it is common sense, but it *does* need to be defined because general maintenance on a home varies more than you may anticipate. General maintenance includes many common, easy tasks that could help you save money in the long run. For example, frequently mopping and cleaning could prevent or defer replacements in a home, therefore saving money.

Some systems need maintenance by rotation. It is good to add alerts to your cell phone or mark your calendar to remember these tasks. Some items will need to be tended to on a less frequent basis than others. For example, keep an eye out for peeling or chipping paint on the exterior of your home. Exterior window trim and frames are areas that are often forgotten. Wood is a very porous material. Worn paint exposes wooden window frames to rain and moisture. This opens the potential for moisture to infiltrate your home. Change filters whenever they are dirty, but at least as often as the beginning of each season. Consider modifying your unit to include a UV light to help eliminate extra impurities that infiltrate the furnace. If you have a sump pump, check or inspect it around the same time each season. Moreover, every season, check the batteries in all smoke detectors and carbon monoxide detectors. Invest in smoke detectors with ten-year tamper-resistant batteries.

Different seasons warrant different approaches to home maintenance. In the summer, most people opt for outdoor activities to pay closer attention to the outside of their homes. I, however, feel that the winter months demand the most attention to prevent costly repairs. Yes, in the summer, the sun is bright and warm, and the outside tends to be more appealing. We want our lawns green and plush, and we love our flowers to be bright and fragrant. However, regarding keeping our homes in order, houses need more attention and maintenance in the winter. In the winter, the potential for issues is greater. Rainwater could potentially dam in the gutters, causing a leak, while fine cracks left unattended in the winter could grow larger from ice. Salt or other granules may need to be applied to driveways to prevent slips and falls or other accidents. Invest in a snow shovel, snow thrower, generator, or another alternative power source for these months. Bread and eggs are not the only items needed when blizzards are forecasted. Some of these items are fueled by gasoline, so stock up on that, too, as winter storms approach. Some jurisdictions have building codes that require interior garage doors and walls to be designed and constructed with special material or drywall that is thicker than normal drywall. The required material is thicker than normal drywall and consists of flame-retardant materials. These materials help insulate and keep carbon monoxide from car exhausts from seeping into the home's interior.

Do you need to hire a contractor?

Please hire contractors who are licensed individuals in your state. Hiring a licensed individual helps protect you and your property. Being licensed ensures that the individual has the knowledge needed to professionally complete your project and lets you know that the individual you hire has undergone a background check. I included some pointers to help you when hiring service personnel for your home or investment. I have chosen the state of Maryland as an example, but you should contact your local Chamber of Commerce or your local labor licensing board for information in your state.

In Maryland, the Department of Labor, Licensing, and Regulation (DLLR) has regulated a specific set of rules, including wording that contractors must use and ethics that must be followed.[8] For example, to protect consumers in Gaithersburg, Maryland, the regulating county's rules are stated on the home-improvement contract. The contract requirements include, but are not limited to, items that assist in preventing disputes. These rules are subject to change at any time, but at the time of publication, it was required that home improvement contracts include many protective clauses. I am sure there are similar rules in most states. Learn your rights. It is smart to know the terms your local lawmakers have mandated for contractors to put in a contract, as those terms could prevent you from landing yourself in court or being a victim of a scam. It could also help you save money. Hire referrals, companies, or individuals who have already done good work for people you know and trust. As always, consult an attorney to help with interpreting or drafting any contract.

UTILITIES

Whenever I hear the word "utility," the first thing I imagine is an expense or bill. Utilities are also just as important as the mortgage. Keeping that in mind, I chose to focus heavily on tips to help you save money and maintain the items in your home to keep them working properly and efficiently. If the appliances in your home operate as designed, not only will they last longer, but they will save energy and money.

There are many ways to maximize saving energy. The larger your home, the more expensive it is to heat, cool, and maintain. One of the ways to save is to purchase energy-saving light bulbs and appliances. Another way is to have your systems checked regularly to ensure that they continue to operate properly over time. A refrigerator with worn trim or broken suction gaps at the door could let air in, causing your refrigerator to run overtime as it struggles to maintain the required cold temperature. Furnaces and air conditioning units operate similarly. If they are not working properly, your home is not being heated or cooled efficiently, costing you additional money. Even faulty, off-track garage doors could allow energy to escape. Most utility companies have energy-saver programs. They will send out a specialist to check your home energy efficiency and issue an energy-efficiency rating. This will pinpoint the areas of your home with possible deficiencies. It is a great idea to utilize this program if your utility company has it available. *Budget programs* average your bills and calculate the average amount on your past billing cycles. This ensures a predictable charge on monthly bills and prevents billing surprises on the months you use more energy. If you transfer your service to a new address, the company may require you to pay the balance of your actual usage before you start service at a new address. At times, some utility companies calculate an estimated bill based on your utility bill average. This estimated bill could be higher if you have recently changed your habits. This higher average could be used to generate your bill instead of your actual usage. If you suspect your bills are too high (or even too low), reach out to your utility company to complete an assessment. If your bill is too low, you may unexpectedly end up with a whopper of a bill. If you live in the western United States, where solar wind and power are more widely used, know that states share power when there is an excess. This helps to save energy and results in less expensive utility bills than eastern states. On the western side of the country, such as California and Arizona, where natural gas is less expensive than electric, most people opt to convert as many utilities as possible to gas from electric, with the unpredictable costs of electric power.

I learned the following ten quick and easy ways to conserve energy and save on utility bills. I like to call these tips my *mini list of home energy life hacks*:

- Wrap your electric water heater in an insulated blanket in the winter to help it quickly warm your water. Be certain to use a safety blanket to prevent fires. Blankets should not be used with gas water heaters with open flames.

- Enclose or shade your air conditioning unit or heat pump to keep it out of direct sunlight to conserve energy. Be sure that your exterior unit stays on a level surface. If the unit tilts or is placed on a hill, it could cause unnecessary wear and tear on the unit.

- Insulate plumbing pipes to help them maintain a steady temperature. Running your hot water for an extended period until it "runs hot" indicates that the pipe is in a location that is cooling the water while not in use.

- Upgrade toilets made before 1992 to newer, "low flow" toilets. These hold less in the bowl and the tank, which means saving money on your water bill.

- Turn the heat or air conditioner off and open your windows as much as possible on cool, nice days.

- Turn off the lights and open blinds during daylight hours to conserve energy.

- If you have a well pump, you will not receive a water bill, but your well pump uses electric power to operate. If you have a leak, your well pump uses energy, which will be included in your energy bills. This also causes wear and tear on your well system. Repair leaks as soon as possible.

- Appliances that heat use more energy than other appliances. When it comes to saving energy, water heaters can be tricky. Most energy-saving tipsters will advise homeowners to lower the temperature of a hot water heater to save money and prevent bacteria growth, but I advise against it. When not in use, your water heater works continuously to heat the water inside and maintain its temperature based on your setting. Lowering the temperature allows the coils to rest, but the lower temperature also allows a petri dish of bacteria to grow. Consider investing in an energy-saving hot water heater system. A tankless water heater is one option. I also suggest installing a heat trap if your unit does not already have one. Bacteria that cause Legionnaires' disease can grow in temperatures between 68°F and 122°F.[9] Setting a higher temperature on the water heater will kill the bacteria. If you have an older tank, service the tank every six months by increasing the temperature to 140°F and then draining the tank to expel the chemicals that have distilled out of the water and settled to the bottom of the tank. Be careful to monitor water usage during this procedure, as 140°F water can cause serious burns in less than five seconds. Water temperatures 135°F and up, among other factors, could increase water pressure buildup in a tank, so have a plumber assist you if you are not familiar with draining or sanitizing a water heater.

- Unplug appliances that are not in use. Cell phone chargers, televisions, lamps, and other devices use phantom energy when turned off. Some devices have auto-standby power mechanisms that cause them to turn on and off at certain intervals. Although those devices use minimal amounts of power, multiple appliances plugged in simultaneously could cause electricity charges to add up unexpectedly.
- Lower the ball or water level adjustment flap in the back of your toilet to adjust the tank's fill to a lower level. This adjustment will allow less water to fill and flush your toilet, thereby lessening your water bill.

Tip: It may seem practical to purchase older, refurbished, or outdated appliances to save money. However, purchasing older and outdated appliances may not help you save at all. In fact, the older the appliance, the more energy it will potentially burn. Older appliances do not meet today's energy-efficient standards. Some may even be recalled after being discovered to be unsafe and having the potential to cause fires.

GO GREEN AT HOME

There are many ways to go green in your home. As discussed previously, most of these ways are conserving energy, but those are not your only options. Going green could involve a lifestyle change, and it does require work. The green lifestyle includes eliminating or lessening the use of harmful chemicals and other non-natural substances in your home. This can be done in many ways. Ten great ideas to start implementing include:

1. Use non-chemical pesticides and cleaning solutions in and around your home. Find ways to use natural products or use live bugs to help you manage your gardens. Ladybugs are great for gardens. Ladybugs are a predator of aphids. Aphids are a type of bug that eats away at vegetables, trees, and different types of plants. Using them is a creative, natural, and inexpensive alternative for lessening the use of chemical pesticides. Ladybugs are just one insect known to seek and kill harmful, soil-dwelling insects. Ladybugs can typically be purchased inexpensively on various sites on the Internet. Using wood-burned ashes is also a great way to naturally reduce insects in your garden because wood ash is an insect repellent. Wood-burned ash turns to lye when mixed with water. Lye is a great slug, snail and bug deterrent.

2. Lessen or eliminate the use of high-wattage electrical appliances or appliances that utilize and emit harmful chemicals or gases. For

example, there are highly effective push lawn mowers that eliminate the use of petroleum gas.

3. Buy products labeled "natural" or "organic." Use products such as white vinegar and scented natural oils as odor eliminators to eliminate emitting chemicals into your environment and body. The EPA released a document[10] that offers great resources and information regarding green cleaning, sanitizing, and disinfecting.

4. Purchase houseplants for the inside of your home. Plants emit natural oxygen into the air that helps us breathe. An article about NASA plant research was published in 2019 and chronicled the NASA Clean Air Study. The article mentions how NASA considers "plants and associated microorganisms in the soil around them "nature's life-support system."[11] There are specific plants that have been studied and found to improve indoor air quality. In addition, some people claim that Himalayan salt lamps have helped clean the air in their homes. It has been stated that these lamps help eliminate tough odors and aid in ridding excess interior air moisture through negative air ionization.[12]

5. Recycle everything possible. There are recycling plants for almost everything. If you need help finding a recycling or removal service, check www.freecycle.org ® to find a service in your area. It is a grass roots movement of people who give and take free stuff locally, helping to keep landfills free of usable items.

6. Eat organic foods. This helps lessen the use of pesticides on crops. For organic food sources in your area, go to www.Eatwellguide.org. Eatwellguide.

org is a directory of over 25,000 restaurants, farms, markets, and other resources offered in the United States. The establishments included in this directory meet a "standard of inclusion". The restaurants and farms, etc are all said to sell and/or serve "sustainable foods", by the organization's interpretation. This is also a nonprofit organization.

7. Use glass plates and utensils instead of paper and plastic.

8. Plant a garden to grow fruits and vegetables. To start, be sure to use non-GMO and organic seeds or plants.

9. Build and use a compost container to dispose of garbage. This will prevent you from buying fertilizers or potting dirt that include heavy chemicals and pesticides. It will also save money on buying potting soil.

10. Invest in solar power. Solar panels are a wonderful way to save on energy costs. You could also use solar powered lawn lights. Be certain to become well informed about possible liens or encumbrances that may be involved regarding solar panel installation or leasing.

UNINVITED GUESTS

I know you probably thought this section would teach you how to keep your in-laws away, but you are not so lucky! This chapter will help you understand how you can keep your home free of pests and most rodents. There are many unsuspecting ways these tiny, uninvited critters enter your home. You may have heard your elders discuss the squirrels in the attic and wondered how they got there. One way is through loose, receded shingles or detached damaged gutters. Yes, squirrels, mice, birds, and snakes can get into your home from outdated, damaged gutters or roof shingles and buckled siding. Unmaintained, old roof shingles can warp, recede, and pull back from the eave, or overlapping area, over your gutters. This causes a gap that almost any critter sees as an invitation inside your home. Gaps in siding, missing, and damaged door or garage trim could also lead to a critter problem.

The winter months are the most common season to discover a rodent problem because your home creates a warm haven from the harshness outside. Their *lives* depend on it. Pest issues, on the other hand, are more common in the spring and summer months. Spring is known as "pest season." Pests include ants, moths, spiders, roaches, beetles, and flies. Any undesirable insects that intrude on your habitat are defined as pests. Holes in screens are a common way in for these pests, but they are very diligent at finding an entrance. Cable or utility lines that lead inside a home from the outside have been a sneaky way for mice to travel into a home to stay warm.

Keep wood trellises, trim, firewood, and mulch away from the foundation of your home. Termites, carpenter ants, and other wood-destroying insects are attracted to dead wood, which does not contain chlorophyll. A study by North Carolina State University mentions:

"Without a periodic inspection of your home, termite activity can remain undetected for years. Some signs of their activity show up unexpectedly, while others are discovered by accident or during renovations."[13]

Many people are terrified of termites. A termite or other wood-destroying insect infestation issue can normally be treated. Discovering that your home has termites does not always mean that you have a huge problem or that you must move.

Tip: If you have pets or small children, try to choose non-toxic, natural products, such as chemical-free or pet-friendly ingredients, to rid the inside and outside of your home from pests. Pets are curious and could easily inhale or eat these items.

TITLE INSURANCE

Title insurance is a policy, predominately found in the United States, which insures against financial loss from claims or liens against real property. Title insurance guarantees that the property is deeded in the rightful owner's name, having the right to sell or otherwise transfer the property to another. The insurance company pays damages to the titleholder or mortgagee to correct discovered problems connected to ownership or title. This insurance normally covers problems that were not discovered or missed by the examiner and errors in public records during a title search. Defects occurring after you moved into your home are not covered. Title insurance is a one-time fee, paid in full, as part of the closing costs. Some states require the seller to cover this cost and give the buyer the option to accept or reject coverage of a policy. For good measure, I suggest that buyers accept coverage. "An ounce of prevention is worth a pound of cure," as the old saying goes.

There are two types of coverage: standard (basic) and enhanced. Inquire with your title or settlement attorney or closer to explain the differences between the two so you can make an informed decision on which policy best suits your needs. The cost may vary per state, so ask questions regarding pricing.

Should you have issues with your title, or if anyone contacts you regarding errors with your deed, title, ownership, or mistakes discovered in your deed's recordation, contact your title insurance policy insurer to file a claim. If you are unsure of what to do, contact the title company where you closed escrow or contact your real estate agent with questions. You should have received title policy information at closing, including your insurance company's name and contact information. Your policy information is especially important. If you have any questions regarding your policyholder or have misplaced your policy information, please ask your closer.

If you own a mobile home, trailer, or manufactured home with wheels, you will be issued a vehicle identification number (VIN). You may rent the land or may have purchased it separately from the owner. It is also possible that you are subject to paying ground rent. Your title will be registered with the local department of motor vehicles. If you need information regarding your unit, you could contact the local police department or state trooper's barracks. If you wish to transfer ownership of your mobile unit, you will need to transfer the title, like transferring the title to a car.

ADDING A SPOUSE/SIGNIFICANT OTHER TO A DEED

Some homebuyers have problems that prevent them from purchasing a home together with a spouse or significant other. It could be because of credit issues, debt, or other personal reasons. It may be possible to add the second person to the deed after closing but be cautious. Recordation and title holdings may vary tremendously.

When there is an existing deed of trust (mortgage), you may have to get permission from the mortgagee to consummate this. In many instances, modifying an existing deed of trust could trigger the due-on-sale or acceleration clause in many mortgages. Read your Mortgage Deed of Trust or Mortgage Note for details on prohibitions. Contact a title company or title attorney, and they can facilitate this type of transaction. If allowed, fees associated with this transaction include, but are not limited to, recordation fees and title fees. There may also be lien certification or lien search performed in which a judgment search is done on the individual(s) being added to the deed. It could be considered a fraudulent practice to add someone without notifying your mortgage servicer. This is because signers were approved as qualified based on their financial capability. Adding or removing an entity to a deed may not relieve the original mortgagor of the responsibility of the debt secured to buy the home. As always, consult an attorney regarding possible legal and financial consequences.

If a cash purchase were made, the owner could add or remove owners to their deed as often as possible, including paying the respective recording fees. Modifying or revising your deed to add a family member could help avoid probate issues in the future, should you die intestate (without a will). As a Certified Probate Real Estate Specialist, I urge you to understand that the way your deed is titled is an especially important topic to discuss with your family, especially if you have not executed a will. Some lives are disrupted, financially and physically, by searching to find documents after a loved one's death, simply because of the way their property is titled and recorded. Being certain to properly exercise this step in your closing could make a huge difference for your family. Contact an attorney or title representative to get more information on how specific title conveyances could better suit your needs. Recording your deed properly and strategically could save you and your family valuable time, stress, and lots of money.

Tip: Legal issues such as ex parte, restraining orders, and incarcerations could trigger a due-on-sale clause. If the deed of trust requires both mortgagors to occupy the premises, but one party is forced out of the home, this could be considered a breach of the deed of the trust instrument.

FINANCIAL ISSUES AFTER BUYING

Contact your local agent or Realtor® if you anticipate a financial hardship. They may be able to help you with finding options or assisting with a short sale, if applicable. Your agent may be able to temporarily rent out your home and manage tenants so you can keep your home and possibly avoid foreclosure. Refinancing may be an option to lower your monthly payment if you have not been late on your payments. Some loans require that you occupy the premises for a specified period, at least initially, after closing. Others mandate that you occupy the home for the duration of your loan. There may be a deed or deed of trust limitations on what can be done with your property. If your property is in a senior or 55+ community, condominium, or coop, there may be specific limitations or rules governing your choices. If your hardship is temporary, you may be able to move back into your home once you re-establish your finances.

There are possible ways to attempt to lessen your expenses after closing. One way to save on your mortgage payment is to have your private mortgage insurance (PMI) removed if you have a conventional loan. Policies constantly change, but at the time of publication, there were provisions to have your PMI removed for mortgages closed after July 29, 1999.[14] Once your equity reaches 20% of your original appraised value, you can request to have the monthly PMI removed. There are, however, stipulations for approval. To start the process, submit a written request. Some lenders require a good payment history by the homeowner. The lender may also require you to certify that no junior liens or second mortgages exist on the home. An appraisal may be required to prove evidence of the equity if it is suspected that the home's value has significantly changed. This removal process should be automatic, without request, once your principal balance reaches 78% of the original value of your home. However, you must be current on the payments on the anticipated cancellation date. If you have the required equity but are not current on your payments, the PMI will be terminated after your payments are brought to date. For FHA-insured mortgage holders, it is wise to contact your mortgage servicer to see if you qualify for the reduction or removal of your mortgage insurance. The answer varies based on your mortgage origination date, your loan balance, and mortgage status. You can also contact the Consumer Financial Protection Bureau.

Shop around for a less expensive homeowner's insurance policy. Bundling home and auto insurance policies are a great way to reduce expenses. Try bundling utilities, too. Home and cell phone companies and cable, TV, and Internet providers frequently offer subscribers discounts to combine all your services into one company. Applying for senior, disability, military, and other tax breaks or exemptions could be good options if you qualify.

Consider getting a second job or roommate if you begin to struggle financially. Use your talents to produce online podcasts or consider offering classes for a fee. Online freelancing is great for boosting your finances. Consider using your unique talents to offer sales or services on web apps or sites like Fiverr, Esty, and other similar freelance platforms. Do you own an RV that may be collecting dust in your yard? Put it to use by renting it out to make extra cash. Be certain to check with your local regulatory agency regarding pertinent laws involving RV/mobile rentals to avoid violating any rules in your area. Do you have a drone camera that you use for fun? Try to employ your services to local real estate agents who may need aerial views of homes or occupancy checks in areas that they may not want to visit themselves. Always inform your mortgage company as soon as possible if you foresee being late on your mortgage payments. Do not ignore their calls or letters. They may be willing to assist you in a temporary hardship.

WHAT IF I HAVE A REVERSE MORTGAGE?

A reverse mortgage is a mortgage loan that is available to borrowers aged 62 and older. The mortgage is secured by residential property and allows the borrower to convert equity payments into cash upfront. In a regular mortgage, you make payments every month. In a reverse mortgage, the lender makes payments *to you*. When you die, surviving heirs can sell the property to recoup any equity there is left. Many families of reverse mortgage owners do not understand what to do when their family members die. Please inform family members or heirs as soon as possible if you have a reverse mortgage. Instruct them on how to proceed with settling your affairs, including instructions on how to handle your property. Death of a sole mortgagor triggers the due-on-sale clause, meaning the lender must be repaid. If there are two mortgagors (for example, both mom *and* dad) the surviving spouse can continue living in the home with the mortgage unchanged. Normally, a clause is attached to reverse mortgages that give family members a specified time to sell their deceased family member's property after death. These actions run on a strict timeline. Heirs can apply for a maximum of two 90-day extensions. The lender must approve extensions with documented extenuating circumstances and active diligence showing attempts to sell the home or satisfy the balance. During this period, interest continues to accrue, and insurance balances remain due that will eat away at the home's equity. Note – lenders keep track of databases noting deaths, and they are aware of the date when the clock starts ticking. Do not attempt to buy time by thinking the lender may be unaware of your loved one's passing. Lack of notification does not save time on the six-month allotted time to sell. These terms may vary depending upon your mortgagor, so please review your documents with an attorney.

WHAT IF I NEED TO SELL?

If you need to sell your home, please call a real estate agent you trust. The National Association of Realtors® defines a Realtor® as a registered collective membership mark that identifies a real estate professional who is a member of the National Association of Realtor® and subscribes to its strict Code of Ethics.[15] Some professionals have loosely adapted this term over the years and use its brand to identify real estate professionals. Real estate professionals or agents licensed and certified to use the Realtor® designation must belong to one or more of the 1,700 local associations/boards and over 54 state and territory associations. Realtors who remain a part of this association bind themselves to loyalty to clients, cooperation with competitors, the fiduciary duty to clients, truthfulness in statements and advertising, and non-interference in exclusive relationships that other Realtors® have with their clients. You can choose any agent to represent you but choosing for integrity is always the best choice.

Once you contact your chosen real estate agent, they should assess your needs and explain the next steps. After the housing and financial crash we faced in the last decade, life is much different. If your agent has been out of the industry for an extended period, ask questions to decide if this agent still possesses the experience needed to assist you with your transaction. The real estate industry has evolved over the years and continues to change. Without constant training and experience, your agent may not be aware of the many avenues needed to meet your goals. The once solely used closing document, the HUD 1, has been replaced in some transactions.

Moreover, the old basic loan process used to prepare customers and clients to expect financially is much longer. An agent must be knowledgeable and well-versed to introduce a buyer and seller to realistic expectations. Now, much more is done electronically, and there are rules regulating that seemingly small part of a transaction. Be honest when communicating your needs to your agent, and I'm sure they will handle the rest with the utmost perseverance, integrity, and care.

WHAT IF I DON'T HAVE EQUITY?

If you need to sell, immediately contact your real estate agent. They can determine if you need to pursue a short sale based on certain factors involving your local market, needs, and financial situation. In this type of sale, the mortgage company allows a homeowner to modify their original promise of the mortgage and pay them back less than what they owe; therefore, shorting the bank. You may have equity and not even know about it! A short sale is not guaranteed. Therefore, they are labeled, *potential short sales* in some multiple listing services. Some procedures must be followed to consummate a successful short sale transaction and variables uniquely affecting each deal. Short selling involves your mortgagee in your sale as a third-party approver, and they must agree with terms executed in a contract between you and a buyer. Your agent, negotiator, and possibly other entities will need written authorization to discuss your sale with your mortgage company. This is a much more complex transaction than a regular sale of a home with equity, and it often takes an extended period to close, that is, *if* it closes. Most sellers in a short sale must have a viable reason for the mortgagee to approve a short sale. This normally includes a financial hardship or life catastrophe. These reasons must be documented. In my career, deaths of a major wage earner, divorce, and disability have been some hardships approved for short sales. Each sale and lender are unique, with a unique set of guidelines and procedures for short sales.

When you were qualified and approved for a mortgage, you did all you could to prove and document that you were a viable, able purchaser. In a short sale, you must prove why you are no longer in that same financial position as when you initially purchased. If you possess funds such as a 401k, thrift savings, or other liquefiable assets, the mortgage company could consider those funds as applicable to the payoff in some way. This could be required as a signed promissory note at closing, or as a condition for third party sale approval. Most buyers and sellers state that the time invested in closing a short sale is the biggest deterrent. In the past, some lenders offered incentives to homeowners to make a short sale instead of property abandonment or foreclosure. Those incentives are becoming rare. Currently, I predict that short sales could become extinct as time passes and the real estate market continues to strengthen and regains momentum since the crash. Do not sit on the fence if you feel you may need to utilize this option, as you may lose the ability to do so as time passes. If you are a seller and you pursue a short sale, here is a brief list of pointers that could help you shorten your process and close faster:

1. Gather the past two years of tax returns and your most recent W2 for your mortgage company. Be responsive to their requests.

2. Prepare a written hardship statement explaining your hardship, documenting a disability, or explaining your loss of employment.
3. Prepare your home to be shown. *This means to clean out and spruce up your home. Expensive repairs are not necessary.*
4. Agree to allow an agent to list your home with a price in line with your area's market.
5. Agree to allow a lockbox to be placed on the home so it can be easily shown. It is extremely important that buyers can gain access to the home.
6. Allow professional photos to be taken. Buyers love 360-degree virtual tours.
7. Allow a sign to be placed in the yard.
8. Answer your phone and communicate with your lender if they contact you. Ignoring calls only lengthens the process and may cause a rejection of your short sale.

Not adhering to these points could potentially cause a delay in this type of transaction. If you document a hardship to sell for less than what is owed, the bank wants to see that you are diligently attempting to sell quickly for the most money. They want to know if you are actively marketing the home.

Do you have a *for-sale* sign up?

Is your home actively listed on the market?

They also want to know the agent who has the home listed for sale, including the agent's contact information. A short sale requires diligence on the seller's part as well as on the buyer's. Buyers of a short sale are often required to show proof of funds and give personal information to the short sale bank to prove they are eligible and ensure that the transaction is arm's length. Arm's length means that the buyer and seller are not closely related family members. It also means that there is no existing business relationship or conflict of interest. The bank is aware of homeowners who try to defraud their system by selling to a relative so the mortgagor can remain in the house. Some lenders allow arm's length transactions; some are strictly opposed to them. Most lenders have information online regarding their process for attempting a short sale.

SECURITY

Traditional security systems in your home are great, but they are mostly self-explanatory. In this chapter, I discuss a different type of security to help keep you safe. I am sharing information about a lesser-known transgression that you may take for granted. Yes, I am happy to know that you are excited about your purchase, and I like hearing about great accomplishments in life. You posted your nice, expensive, new designer purse and shoes on your social media accounts to show your great sales month, but you also made yourself a target. It is a bad idea to post valuables and possessions on social media. Posting your every move and whereabouts are also bad practices. Even though I'm glad to see everyone get an opportunity to relax, it's a bad idea to notify everyone you know (and those you don't) that you will be vacationing in Bermuda for two weeks. This makes you a potential target for burglary. Protecting your family and investment involves making smart decisions, even when it entails keeping some of your business to yourself. Nosey friends are not the only ones watching. Hackers and identity thieves no longer find their treasures solely by going through your trash at your curb. These criminals piece together as much as they can about you from the comfort of their homes, via the Internet, to rob you. The more you reveal about yourself in different surveys, applications, and websites, the more vulnerable you become. It is important to dispose of sensitive documents at your home but be mindful and aware of your online trash, too. Government safety organizations state, "Burglars can make use of techniques usually employed by stalkers to determine when your house and possessions are most vulnerable."[16] Some may not be aware that their activities are open to vulnerabilities. Sometimes it isn't always us who leaks the information about our daily lives. To be safe, we must monitor our kids' Internet traffic to be certain they are not the ones sharing details of our lives for the world to see.

Even something as seemingly harmless as taking a picture and posting it to an app or website could allow everyone in cyberspace to track your location and link those pictures to usernames on other online applications. There are hidden data attached to pictures called EXIF data. EXIF data shares information about the photo sharer, and some data storage even allows reverse image searches. When removing this data, you won't always strip the outside world of other data that can be revealed about you just by posting a photo. Suppose you have a gathering at your home and someone checks in on certain apps. In that case, they are giving strangers their global positioning, therefore, providing *your address*. Socialnomic.net published an article[17] stating, "81% of Internet-initiated crime involves social networking sites…"

It also stated: "More than one million people become victims of cyber-crime every single day, and the financial cost of cyber-crime is larger than the black market for cocaine, heroin, and marijuana combined."

Play it safe and be as careful as possible to protect your privacy. Create fake security answers for passwords and answers to security questions that could be commonly known. For example, instead of using your mother's real maiden name, create a fictitious name that you can easily remember in place of the correct one. At one time, I would tell you to avoid opening emails from people you don't know, but now I say to avoid the quick, second-hand nature of opening emails even from those you *do* know. Hover over the name or email address to verify the email is from the person you believe it to be. Double-check with companies after receiving links to change your password or requests to update information. Call the company to verify that the email is legitimate. Hackers can now create emails and links that closely resemble actual sites, so be careful. Remember to shut your computer down when not in use and be certain you do not have your remote power, wake ability or LAN setting turned on. Invest in good spyware and antiviral software to help protect your activities from being violated. Consider using a Virtual Private Network (VPN) to surf the web. Using a VPN is a good way to hide your Internet activity and browsing data from other WIFI users. This makes it more difficult for your activity and important data to be tracked. VPNs add a layer of security over insecure networks by replacing your IP address with a virtual one. It extends a private network across a public one. Consider obtaining a virtual card number from your credit card company to make online purchases.

Another safety precaution is to change your checking or bank account numbers after you close on your home. Think about when you were making offers to buy your home. You may have made many offers while competing against multiple offers, or maybe you bought the first and only home you offered. Most likely, you wrote a check (or many checks) for your earnest money deposit during this process. This means that your account number on your check has crossed many hands and was possibly seen by many eyes. Purchasing money orders or cashier's checks for earnest money deposits is a good practice when making offers. You probably had to hand over bank statements or other documents, including your social security number, to solidify your loan. This information could have been compromised, too. I am not stating that your financial institution or real estate agent isn't trustworthy. I am simply stating that others could have inadvertently seen your information, and you and your lender may be unaware. Err on the side of caution and change your account information after closing. I offer the same advice to sellers. If you are a seller processing a short sale, this information is most likely required to process your deal. Redact part of your account numbers on your bank statements to keep your financial information private. Many lenders use secure sites to gather and share proprietary information within real estate transactions to enhance privacy for all parties.

YOUR HOME IS YOUR CASTLE

Buying a home has long been labeled part of "The American Dream." This is because buying real estate is the largest, most expensive decision most people make in a lifetime. Regardless of the size of your home, your move is a huge accomplishment. Not only are you buying a structure to build memories, but you are also establishing wealth by making an investment. Your home does not have to be a mansion or have the newest décor when you buy it. It's okay to customize your home by doing small projects one at a time. This is part of making a home *yours*. Do not be intimidated by identifying minor issues or by doing DIY small repairs in your home.

Additionally, if you are a woman, do not let being female discourage you from learning. Empower yourself to do things on your own. I am a woman, and I wrote this book. You, too, can do whatever you want, including maintaining your own home.

Some home purchases are investment-driven from the start. These buyers purchase homes for the investment benefits, and their job is to buy, rehab, and sell before moving on to the next investment when the time is right. Most of these homes are immediately worth more, with a little bit of new carpet, paint, and elbow grease. An old saying goes, "one man's trash is another man's treasure." There is someone who wants to buy almost every home if the price and terms are right.

Land is a high commodity because it cannot be made (well, rarely, anyway). Unless a few major volcanoes erupt and form new land, such as how Hawaii was formed, the land will continue to be scarce. As the population grows, more homes will need to be built. This is the effect of supply and demand. This is why major cities such as New York City and Miami have such high, demanding home and land prices. According to national reports, the U.S. economy has been stimulated all over the country, and home prices are slowly but steadily appreciating in most areas. With that information, you should know that it was a wise decision to choose to buy now.

Whatever your motivation may have been for buying a home, *congratulations!* You have begun your journey into homeownership at a great time and in a great market. This is a wonderful moment, a moment worth celebrating! I'm sure you will enjoy the freedom of owning versus renting, especially if you are saving. Some buyers discover that owning a home is a smaller out-of-pocket payment per month than paying rent. I always tell potential buyers, when you are renting, you are paying a mortgage, but the mortgage is not yours; it is someone else's. Owning a home is cutting out the middleman and paying your mortgage *for less*.

This may not be your first home. You may have moved up or downsized. Regardless, I'm sure the information in this book has shed light on subjects you have wondered about but were afraid to ask. Many of my past clients have thanked me for reminding them during their transaction not to allow anyone who is not part of their purchase contract to interfere or meddle in their thought process while in the decision-making stage of buying a home. If a buyer has lots of outside interference, they need to be reminded who will be solely responsible for the mortgage and the upkeep and who must be comfortable with the purchase once they close. A buyer should never allow someone else to intimidate them or coerce them into purchasing a larger home than they could comfortably manage to maintain to be boastful. Maintaining a home is not as hard as some make it seem. Do small repairs, little by little, pay attention to what is happening with your home, and do general maintenance along the way. These steps keep your home in order. Don't worry; if your agent is anything like me, you can call them at any time with questions regarding your home purchase, even if it was years ago! Many of my clients and customers have become lifelong friends. *Congratulations again, and welcome to homeownership!*

REFERENCES

1. U.S. Fire Administration, FEMA, (2021)
Choosing and Using Fire Extinguishers
https://www.usfa.fema.gov/prevention/outreach/extinguishers.html

2. United States Environmental Protection Agency. (n.d.). *Consumer confidence reports: find your local CCR.* Tools for Community Water Systems.
https://ordspub.epa.gov/ords/safewater/f?p=ccr_wyl:102

3. American Ladder Institute. (2018, March 5). The numbers don't lie: make ladder safety a priority. American National Standards Institute.
https://blog.ansi.org/2018/03/ladder-safety-priority-statistics-ali-ansi/

4. United States Environmental Protection Agency. (2016, July). *Basic radon facts.*
https://www.epa.gov/sites/production/files/2016-08/documents/july_2016_radon_factsheet.pdf

5. United States Federal Emergency Management Agency. (n.d.). *Dealing with mold and mildew in your flood-damaged home.* https://www.fema.gov/pdf/rebuild/recover/fema_mold_brochure_english.pdf

6. American Lung Association, the American Medical Association, the U.S. Consumer Product Safety Commission, and the U.S. Environmental Protection Agency. (2015, January). *Indoor air pollution: an introduction for health professionals.* https://www.epa.gov/sites/production/files/2015-01/documents/indoor_air_pollution.pdf

7. National Renewable Energy Laboratory. (2005, July). *Biodiesel - Clean, green diesel fuel.* https://afdc.energy.gov/files/pdfs/30882.pdf

8. Maryland Department of Labor Licensing and Regulation. (n.d.). *Maryland home improvement contracts.* https://www.dllr.state.md.us/license/mhic/mhicontracts.shtml

9. United States Department of Labor. Occupational Safety and Health Administration. Legionellosis (Legionnaires' Disease and Pontiac Fever). Conditions Promoting *Legionella* Growth and Most Susceptible Water Systems. https://www.osha.gov/legionnaires-disease/hazards

10. UCSF Institute for Health & Aging, UC Berkeley Center for Environmental Research and Children's Health, Informed Green Solutions, and California Department of Pesticide Regulation. Green Cleaning, Sanitizing, and Disinfecting: A Toolkit for Early Care and Education, University of California, San Francisco School of Nursing: San Francisco, California, 2013. https://www.epa.gov/sites/production/files/documents/ece_curriculumfinal.pdf

11. SPINOFF. NASA. (2019). NASA Plant Research Offers a Breath of Fresh Air.
https://spinoff.nasa.gov/Spinoff2019/cg_7.html

12. Maurer, H. (2016). *Khewra Salt Mines*
Global Geography.
https://globalgeography.org/af/Geography/Asia/Pakistan/Special_Information/Khewra_Salt_Mines

13. Waldvogel, M. and Alder, P. (2017, June 20). *Termites: biology and control.* NC State extension publications. https://content.ces.ncsu.edu/termites-biology-and-control

14. United States Department of Housing and Urban Development. (n.d.). *Discontinuing monthly mortgage insurance premium payments.* Mortgagee Letter, 2000-46. https://www.hud.gov/program_offices/housing/comp/premiums/prem2001

15. National Association of Realtors. (2017). *Code of ethics and standards of practice of the national association of realtors®.* https://www.nar.realtor/sites/default/files/policies/2017/2017-Code-of-Ethics.pdf

16. United States Federal Bureau of Investigation. (n.d.). *Internet social networking risks.* https://www.fbi.gov/file-repository/internet-social-networking-risks-1.pdf/

17. Hendricks, D. (2014). *The shocking truth about social networking and crime.* Socialnomics. https://socialnomics.net/2014/03/04/the-shocking-truth-about-social-networking-crime/

ABOUT THE AUTHOR

Shea C. Johnson has been a Realtor® in the D.C, Maryland, and Virginia area for over 24 years. Shea is an associate broker, licensed Maryland home improvement contractor, and owns a property management firm. She has worked and invested in many different facets of the real estate industry, with a concentration in the foreclosure, REO, and distressed sale industries. Saturation in these vastly different platforms of the real estate industry has allowed Shea to list, sell, preserve, manage, and evaluate homes in all conditions and all types of communities — urban, suburban, rural, and water-oriented communities. Shea, a native Washingtonian, has lived in the DMV area all her life and continues to reside in Maryland with her husband and three children.

APPENDIX

Seasonal Cheat Sheet

Winter	Spring Daylight savings – set clocks forward one hour	Summer	Fall Daylight savings – set clocks back one hour
Change furnace filters	Change furnace filters	Change furnace filters	Change furnace filters
Winterize your home. Test well water quality	Change batteries in smoke/carbon monoxide detectors	Manage grading	Change batteries in smoke/carbon monoxide detectors
Have an energy assessment performed	Have septic system drained	Inspect foundation	Inspect exterior grading
Check for openings to prevent critters		Have an energy assessment performed	Get an annual HVAC system check
Close off all water lines not in use. Insulate all exposed pipes			

www.LifeAfterClosing.com

For more useful tips and information, please visit this book's website. Feel free to register to be a part of my blog and ask questions related to topics in this book. Congratulations, again, on your home purchase, and thank you for reading!

Please send permission requests to:
P.O. Box 345
Brandywine, Maryland 20613

www.ingramcontent.com/pod-product-compliance
Lightning Source LLC
Chambersburg PA
CBHW070046120526
44589CB00035B/2359